# THE IN-POWERED WOMAN

### A GUIDE TO ACTIVATING AND MATERIALIZING YOUR PERSONAL POWER

## NIKKIE PRYCE

Nikkie Pryce Contact Information :
Email: Nikkie@Nikkiepryce.com
Website: Nikkiepryce.com

Published by Live Limitless Authors Academy & Publishing Co.
Publishing@sierrarainge.com

Printed in the United States of America
Cover Design by: Live Life Creative
Cover Photo by: Mackinley Spex Photo Madhere

ISBN: 978-1-970079-74-6
Library of Congress Number: 2019918034

# DEDICATION

To any woman or person reading this and has a desire
to change their life.

This one's for you.

# CONTENTS

# ACKNOWLEDGMENTS

I acknowledge Jesus for his never-ending grace and favor for me. I honor my mother Naomi Morrison (RIP) and my father Garfield Pryce for giving me the gift of life. Thank you to my family and my friends. To my book publisher Sierra, for encouraging me through this process and helping me to finish strong. To my friend first, Harold, thank you for always believing in me. Love you all forever.

# THE IN-POWERED WOMAN

# Introduction

In this book, I will help you discover how transformative it is to face trauma and to then transition from tragedy into triumph. This book is a tool to help you explore how you can take the cards that you were dealt, and win big even when it seems as if the cards are stacked against you. Seriously, you've picked up this book for one or two reasons.

One, you probably immediately fell in love with the photo, font or color selection on this book or you're a woman who wants to fall madly in love with her greater more powerful self.

Either reason, is amazing and if you stay a bit longer, I can explain why you should stay here for good and what you'll get out of our encounter together. I am 99.9% sure that you're wondering what an IN-Powered woman even means and how does this "term" apply to you.

Well, this simple yet effective term means to be a woman who is empowered enough to know how powerful she is. Simple, right? See personal power, especially as a woman, happens from within first. There are a series of steps that you can take to feel the fulfillment that you have been yearning for. Let's start with some research, shall we? According to a published article on the Huffpost, 1 out of 4 women suffer with low confidence.

If you fall within this category, this alarmingly high statistic is affecting your family, finances, and your career. When there is a lack of inner belief in one's self, and abilities, we tend to fall short in many other areas. This includes our mental health and our money. C'mon somebody! As women, we are so proficient in producing; you give us a seed, and we take that seed and produce much fruit, give us flour and we can turn it into bread. Give us a house and we can create a home.

We are master creators. Our power resonates with the ultimate Master Creator who spoke the entire universe into existence. Talk about innovation and creativity! Every single thing that we desire to create as women, we are able to do. I also feel and understand that we have the personal power to heal ourselves, our sisters, our families and our communities.

My greatest desire is to not only encourage,

motivate and allow you to have moments of laughter, but to inspire you to do more of the work required to ignite a catalyst of change in your life first and then for others. We all know that anytime we board an aircraft, during the flight, the attendants always forewarn us that if the plane decides to take a sudden turn for the worse, to please put on your mask before you try to put anyone else's mask on.

Isn't this how life is? During chaos, we tend to suppress, or run from our own issues instead of taking time to sort through our own internal challenges. We want to attempt to "fix" everyone else's stuff. Well, this book is an indicator that it's time for you to get your house in order. Queen, there is no way that you will be useful to anyone until you get your life together first.

Once, I sat in a session with my therapist, and I recall how groggy the walls looked from the outdated paint. I remember how cold I felt that day because the A/C was blasting so vigorously. Or was it that I had become cold from all of my life experiences that I was attempting to get a hold of.

I can remember the intensity of my heart pounding in my chest as I fought to hold back tears. I wanted to bellow in sorrowful sobbing, but my relentless attitude, and my interior wall of strength wouldn't allow me to release. Across from me sat, my black therapist.

This woman was probably in her mid 30's, with long dreadlocks that she styled neatly in a tight knotted bun. I stared this black woman in her face and she said words to me that I didn't know would impact me so greatly. She said, "you see, the thing about grief is, it will show its ugly face at the most inconvenient of times."

And boy was she right! We can hide, we can wear masks, pretend that we are alright and nothing seems to be bothering us, or pretend that we aren't being affected by our life's inconvenient moments, but I will tell you this Queen, no amount of makeup can make-up for the years of allowing unsettled issues to take root in your life. It creates a flourishing oak tree of deception along with suppressed pain and agony.

I understand sis, and that's why I am on assignment to help you break through from what you've been through, so that you can move forward to where you're going. You see, I can keep your secrets. You know the ones, that if a soul knew, you would melt in despair. I can keep those secrets because it has happened to women all around this country.

Some of it has even happened to me, which I will share later. Though this book is written with the Christian woman of faith in mind, this book is available and open to anyone who has a pulse and can take what this book approaches and then apply it to their lives. Look at this book as a fish. When you steam a fish for dinner, immediately, you'll eat the meat and leave the bones.

If there's some information in here that doesn't apply to you, that's alright. Leave it there, just like you would the fish bones. But, if you see a scrumptious piece of meat between these pages, take your time to chew it, but, please make sure you devour its content. Though we may have different beliefs and thoughts, we are truly one in the same person. Having similar life experiences at different times.

My next point covers a scripture that I was reading this morning. I read in the bible Ecclesiastes 1:9 (NLT)-History merely repeats itself. It has all been done before. Nothing under the sun is truly new. So, I know you feel like you're alone and you have no one else to run to and you want to quit because no one understands, but listen to me, you're not alone.

We all have some sort of thorn in our flesh as Paul discussed in 2 Corinthians 12 that irritates the life out of us and if we could only assassinate and put it out of its misery, we would be fine and life would all make sense.

However, this isn't how life works and I want to

make this process crystal clear to you. When we first identify what the issue is, we need to face it head on. Grab it by the root and dismantle it by the core. This all boils down to doing the inner soul-work. If you will come on this journey with me, I'd like to help you foresee your future.

Not only from a prophetic standpoint but, by making intentional, strategic adjustments to designing life your way and on your own terms. This manifesto will turn your seemingly intangible ideas and innovations for your life into beautiful and impactful moments that you can carry with you along your journey.

It's life-changing to see what you can become once you do the work required to experience a life change. But, this time, you get it done with the "how-to" versus just the "what." By the time you're finished reading this book, I want you to feel inspired, empowered, and equipped to become a woman who is ready to trust in her own personal power.

It is my hope that you discover the power that resonates within you, and you realize that your ability to do big things was within you all along. As dreamers, we will take action and see the fruit of our labor manifest right before our eyes.

The results will not only be fascinating, but an indication that you're on the right track to a more resourceful, fulfilling, joyful and resilient life. Take the passenger seat while I hop in the driver's seat, buckle up and take this journey with me as we travel down the road of new levels and manifested blessings. You'll see how much meaning your life has and how you can live in this power starting now. You have probably felt like you're powerless in some instances. You may feel, "well who will listen to me? I feel helpless, I really can't make much of a difference, I don't have a voice."

If this applies to you, allow me to bestow upon you, the idea that you are a master creator, made in the image of the ultimate Master Creator. Scripture tells us— "And I will give you the keys of the Kingdom of Heaven. Whatever you forbid on earth will be forbidden in heaven, and whatever you permit on earth will be permitted in heaven." Matthew 16:19.

Your keys are your words. When you open your mouth, you're creating environments and manifesting new worlds into existence. If only you knew how powerful you are. You would probably be more mindful of what you're saying on a daily basis. As soon as it leaves your mouth, you're creating and manifesting it. Well, where do these words come from in the first place? Oh, yeah, it's your thoughts.

"Watch your thoughts, they become your words.

*Watch your words, they become actions. watch your actions, they become habits, watch your habits, they become your character, watch your character, for it becomes your destiny."*

—Lao Tzu

Finally, I want to encourage you to remember that you stand as a source of inspiration, as an example for women and little girls around the world of how strength and vulnerability are linked together. We get to acknowledge each other and grow together. We get to exemplify that women don't have to tear each other down to be heard. We get to be present and see what our deeper challenges are and work through them together.

When we access this internal power, we foster and nurture a world of future generations who understand that their existence matters, and that we have each other's back. That we can come to one another for love and support and that we get to create a world that is sustainable and enlightened. We create a world of IN-Powered women.

# 1
## Who is the IN-Powered Woman?

*"I AM a woman who is empowered and standing in my power to change the world!"*

*"She is healed, she is favored, she is a Queen, she is royalty. She is you."*

You may be asking what is an IN-Powered woman and how can you become one? It sort of sounds like a luxury purchase at a high-end store. Let me get one of these, one of those and an IN-Powered woman on the side, please! Well, this doesn't work like that. However, I will break down how it does work.

An IN-Powered woman knows she's been through life's challenges and back. She has been up against some of the most thrilling times in her life and still has made it through. Her back has been against the wall, she's been overlooked, she's been through life's toughest experiences and she has had to overcome life's struggles. She's done all of this with a smile. She is the one that knows that she is great and is tapping into her greatness daily. She knows that the next woman isn't her competition. In fact, she is ready to show up and support others and make their dreams come true. She knows that when she helps others dreams come true, that hers are on the horizon.

She doesn't hang on to or internalize mistreatment or even rejection from others. She knows her value and she is sure that she is enough. The IN-Powered woman is vulnerable, open, loving and still believes in a life full of love and light regardless of what she's faced with.

She smiles through the storm, knowing that in order to get to it, she has to go through it. The wilderness seasons of her life has taught her character, integrity, grit, love and a winning mentality.

She is power. You see this type of woman isn't perfect. She also isn't the woman who thinks that she must wear a superwoman cape at all times. She knows when to push and when to pause. She loves hard in spite of failed relationships. She knows that fairy tale love may not always be her story.

Sometimes, love for her looks messy, upsetting, devastating, full of tears, and sometimes disappointment but she knows she aspires to feel every facet of emotions required to navigate through the rough plains to true unconditional love.

She understands that she is open to be free and can find pieces of herself in others, her community and the world. She bends but never breaks.

When she takes a hit, she gets back up and musters up the strength to take another swing in the ring. She believes in God. The almighty savior, Jesus. She knows that He was the greatest example of wholeness and goodness. You see, she knows that her power comes from being all that she is and wants to be.

She believes that her voice is impactful and can truly change a generation if she kept her mind and spirit open to the shift that we all need. She will go forth and before anyone else to show others that a true leader stands the test of time and isn't afraid to go through the fire to create the fuel for someone else's boat to sail. She is the epitome of grace and understanding. She gets it. She listens in order to learn from others and she casts aside her judgments to hear someone else out.

She makes mistakes, gets angry, goes into the darkest places of her life to pull out her victories and show others how to do the same. This woman is poised, articulate, sensitive, kind yet assertive. She knows what she wants and doesn't waste her time on anything less than. She is a beauty. The apple of your eye. She walks into a room and her presence alone turns heads. People know when she has arrived, they can sense and feel her spirit. She is a bad mamma jamma. Her body and looks alone breaks every rule. She is the one any man wants to take home to mama. She has to be reminded of her own power at times because she is the essence of power. She at times, needs to be encouraged as well. Check on your strong friend, is a line in her Instagram Bio. She is the strong friend to many.

At times she just needs someone to be strong for her. You see the IN-Powered woman holds this title not because of how much money she has, the accolades she possesses or how fine she is; she holds this title because she's been through it and back and still finds a way to express gratitude to God who she knows has covered her in His amazing grace.

Her heart is open to loving people and she understands the importance of loving herself. She has found a way deep down inside of her to love others and just simply support them. I love this woman. I love her because she is me. She is you. We are her. We have grown so much over the years and at times, with tears in our eyes we appreciate every single moment that God has allowed us to go through.

We are grateful for everything. We are victorious. With our heads held high, we are the women that others can look up to because we have learned the art of letting go in order to love again. You see this woman, I had to become. I had to learn to embrace and accept her for all that she is. I had to learn that she is different, quirky, loud at times yet, sweet, sensitive, fun and inspiring. I have fell madly in love with her. My heart clings to her like a newborn does when they open their eyes for the first time and see their Mommy. I feel so connected to this woman, I know her, I've studied her needs, her deep desires, her fears and her power.

As I evolved into a deeper empowered version of myself, I had to understand that it's alright to see myself where and who I was before. Though there were decisions in my life that I wasn't proud of, I know I can look back and accept that those moments were a part of my beautiful, chaotic, wild, fun and amazing journey.

At times, we look back at our lives and just want to destroy the past version of ourselves. We want to get rid of the memories that lie dormant in our souls, so we suppress everything that has happened to us. Who we were, what we did and what others did to us. However, if we can look back and offer forgiveness and support to ourselves, we can truly see that if it wasn't for those times, life wouldn't be what it is now.

So, to each person who can't see their power, or may not be in a position to own it, it's alright. Sometimes, it takes a moment, to identify who you are and the value and worth you bring into the world. The best part about this is that you get to create what you're choosing to bring into this world. It's all up to you. There's truly beauty in this new beginning. I feel that this is an evolutionary process. You don't just wake up and BOOM, you're an IN-Powered woman.

Nope! You've had to experience and go through some stuff and make it out, to tell your side of the story. I have one word of advice as you're creating this new-found sense of belonging. With each action you make and with every word you speak, you have to consciously understand that you're constantly enrolling people into your belief, mindset, lifestyle and intention.

So, if it's something that you know isn't aiding in the betterment of your life and the lives of those people that you've been called to impact; it's time to reassess where you are and what you're doing. This manual will help you with that. You'll be able to really access what power is, how to own it and how to step into it. It's long overdue if you haven't. Maybe you have already stepped in and owned your power, if that's the case, this book will be an open and vulnerable dialogue with you and I.

I will be sharing my many experiences, in hopes that you can relate and take the many nuggets that I will be dropping along the way. To all of my IN-Powered women out there, past, present and future, let's get on this journey together. Shall We?

# THE IN-POWERED WOMAN

# 2

## Fix the Temporary

*"I AM uprooting anything in my life that no longer serves me."*

On a Friday night, I visited a friend named Raquel. She told me with a soft yet stern voice, "Nikkie you need to take some time to relax." She said this to me as we were partaking in some much-needed girl-talk and I could hear her two sons, in the next room playing games and watching YouTube videos. The words, "relax" some-what triggered me in the moment.

I've heard people ask me if I ever take a moment to just "relax" and as insane as this sounds, I never knew what that looked like for me in my day-to-day experience. At this point, I've been a full-time for entrepreneur for two full years, coming up on my third year. So, I am in a constant state of movement, innovation and creativity.

This mind doesn't turn off. So, my greatest desire
is to initiate more time to relax in a way that
makes sense to me. In this moment, I looked at
my friend, who had the prettiest complexion of
cocoa brown skin, with small slanted eyes, bouncy
natural hair, a dope haircut that would make you
look twice and say, "that's so fly."

Her teeth were aligned with braces that shim-
mered each time she spoke, my friend is a "sista"
who loves God and is funny as heck. Her creative
mind is peculiar, unique and impressive. So, I
wanted her to describe what exactly "relaxing"
looked like. "Just stay home all day and lay in the
bed." She said. I looked at her with the stale face,
saying to myself this will never work.

I thought about the scripture, "lazy people
sleep soundly, but idleness leaves them hungry"
(Proverbs 19:15) and honey, I like to eat, so this
relaxing business was not for me. The moment
that I feel like I'm not effectively producing,
there's an inner guilt that surrounds me and I
push myself to get up and get moving.

However, Raquel was right. I needed to try this
and see how I felt after. Hey, you just never know
what greatness comes out of just being still. I
thanked Raquel for her hospitality, I took in all
of the insight that she shared with me and I made
it to my humble abode. I went to sleep that night
knowing I would be relaxing the next day. The

idea alone made me cringe, however, I wanted to give it a try. The next morning, I awakened from my sleep and headed into the kitchen to make breakfast.

That morning, I made a turkey, egg and tomato breakfast sandwich, with a hot glass of lemon and ginger tea. I was present, quiet and actually appreciating this time I had alone. It was me and God in that moment and it felt really great to be in solitude. It was exclusively designed for me, and that's all that mattered.

Then it started to rain. "Ahhh, this is even more perfect," I thought to myself. I could get some rest while I listened to the raindrops from mother nature, tip-tap on my window pane. I was in heaven, or at least I thought I was. After breakfast, I washed my dishes and headed into my room to lie down. My goal was to probably take a power nap and then maybe read a book and just turn off this creative and brilliant mind of mine. There was only one problem.

I headed into my room, and from a distance right next to my closet door, I saw a circular like black image in my room. Y'all know I'm out here trying to stay saved, but honey whatever that was in my room, made me slip out a word or two that I'm sure my heavenly Father wasn't too pleased with.

Oops, my apologies Daddy. As I walked closer, I

said what is that? Chileeeee, it was a colony of ants on my closet door. Ants! How in the world did ants get into my room? And so many at that? Now, here is my disclaimer. For the ones who instantly thought it, No, I don't eat in my room and my room is for the most part almost always spic and span. I'm rarely home due to working from my office so there isn't much interaction going on there. Plus, I had just cleaned my room days before, so this made no sense to me.

Where did this family of black Ants come from? Anyone who knows me, knows how much I can't stand insects, bugs, and anything that has to slither across the floor to get to its destination. Listen, no shade to anyone who loves nature and all of its insect filled family members, but it's just not my cup of tea. When I saw this, I was bamboozled and petrified.

Immediately I ran to my laundry room and grabbed a bottle of insect spray. For those of you who don't know, when it gets closer to the summer and especially when it rains, bugs are out searching for shelter. For some reason, they found a way in and chose my room. On the day I was supposed to relax, these creepy critters decided to infiltrate my safe space. I wasn't having it.

Now, I know what you're thinking, Nikkie, they are only black ants, it's not a big deal. However,

I don't know about you, but ants shouldn't be in my home having a party at my expense. Next, I saturated the entire colony with insect spray and they instantly fell to the floor. I felt relieved that finally this was being taken care of.

I was raised in a west Indian household. Coming from a Jamaican descent, for some odd reason some of us believe that Bleach can clean anything, and drinking tea will fix any broken bone in your body, we will touch on this another time.

I went back to my laundry room and grabbed the largest bottle of Bleach that I could find. I concocted a formula of bleach, water and a few other products, reassuring myself that this would fix the problem. I cleaned up the area and decided to use my new populated formula to clean the walls, my entire closet floor and my floor in the room. I just knew I was winning.

I took all of my shoes, pumps, heels and boots out of my closet to make sure I caught every nook and cranny in my closet. This was a sure-fire plan that the ants could never return. As I started to clean through my closet, I found a very small hole in the tiling of the floor.

"Eureka!" I yelled. This is where they came through. I just knew I was right. I jumped on the phone with my older guy cousin in Atlanta and he advised me on exactly how to patch up the hole. He sent me on a journey to purchase a bottle of acrylic latex caulk and silicone that I could use to easily seal up the hole and be on my way. I was actually super excited to get this process resolved once and for all. When I arrived back home, I patched up the hole and I was finally at peace and able to rest.

I slept peacefully that night feeling like this was all figured out and at ease. Boy, was I wrong. The next day was pretty normal and my strategies seemed to have fixed the problem. I woke up from my slumber and to my surprise I went to my window sill to see dozens of dead ants on my floor and window sill. It seemed that they couldn't get enough. The formula that I created was only a temporary fix to this nuisance of an issue that is now bringing distress to my life and my day. This is ridiculous.

I didn't understand where these ants were coming from but I said, wow, Nikkie dig deeper. There is a revelation here. This is prophetic. What is God saying to you? I know, I'm deep. As much as I wanted to enter the Holies of Holies with God, I really just wanted these ants out of my way, like right now and I didn't understand why God was allowing this foolishness to take place. That's it I said, I need to call a professional.

My method didn't work and I needed a

professional who could get to the "root" of my problem. You see, I could only see the issue for what it was at the surface, and my response to it was surface as well. This only allowed a more deeply rooted issue to show its ugly face at the most inconvenient of times. At this point, I needed to call around and find someone to help me. My assistant scrambled to find a professional service who could take care of this annoyance.

We finally found someone and they were scheduled to come the next day to assess, treat and monitor the pest problem. I don't know about you, but for me and my house, we shall dwell without creepy crawlers. That night I decided to room with my cousin until the whole ant debacle was over. The next day, I arrived home and waited for pest control to arrive.

When they arrived, they sent a woman out to manage the job. My initial thought was, "Lord, I need this done the right way, why would they send a woman to do this job?" I was so angry and now fuming at this entire situation. I was done. Then, I had a conversation with myself, "Nikkie, allow her to do her job. You need this service, don't allow your frustrations to overtake getting what you need done." She inspected the exterior as well as interior.

When she went into the bathroom, I noticed that her facial expression had changed. When I looked into my shower, there was another colony of ants that had decided to retreat into the bathtub, they were coming up through the drain.

I was disgusted! Wow, this is insane. This is only happening in my bedroom and bathroom. Out of the 4 bedrooms and 2 bathrooms in my home, this is happening in my space. What does this all mean? It ALWAYS means something, we just have to take a moment to connect with God in order to hear what He's saying. The technician was super gracious, funny, and alert but all in all, she was an inspiration.

Wow, she knew exactly where to spray, she walked through the shrubs that's located in my front yard, she found the ant homes which were right outside of my window and she baited and tackled them all. I said, "wow, women are truly magnetic and powerful!" Here I am allowing my frustrations to get the best of me and this woman walks in and conquers the day. I told her how much

I appreciated her and I apologized for my outburst and behavior earlier. She accepted my apology and she guided me through the rest of the entire process. I haven't had a good night's rest for the past few days. Seeking shelter with family until this situation had been rectified, my room being fumigated and feeling like ants were crawling on me was a bit frustrating to say the least.

I was clearly traumatized from it all, but I am now back home in my own space, in my own bed, snoozing the night away without feeling violated by unwanted guests. As I reflect on this entire situation, the question that I pose here is, what is in your life that has infiltrated your safe space? Who is the person, place or thing that you have temporarily put a bandage on and hoped that you could push it far back into your mind so that you could never recall what happened to you?

What have you yet to pull up from the root, but have settled for a temporary fix to soothe your internal wounds? Even though you know that what you merely cover with a bandaid can never heal properly, how long do you allow yourself to suffer before you seek out help? You see this ant situation was brought to me for so much more than to bring me frustration or to attempt to bully me.

It was brought to me to help me recognize what areas in my life that I had temporarily patched up, had failed to address and hadn't gotten to the root of. These were the issues responsible for my silent frustration; and if I didn't take care of it now, it would cost me big time in the near future. I want you to take a moment to evaluate your situation. I encourage you to do a self-assessment so that you can come face to face with any trauma that's lingering around.

What haven't you identified that is possibly causing you more pain internally than you're expressing outwardly? "Take a lesson from the ants, you lazybones. Learn from their ways and become wise! Though they have no prince, governor or ruler to make them work, they labored hard all summer, gathering food for the winter."
(Proverbs 6:6-8 NLT) This reminds me of how much we need to pay attention to the life of the ants.

They don't need anyone to guide them through life, they just do what they were designed to do. They aren't lazy with their struggle, problems or their trauma. They get it done by actively moving in unison with one another and making the necessary adjustments.

Tree roots are pretty deep. So, sometimes, up-rooting situations out of our lives will take time, patience, gentleness and consistent action. There is a misconception that we are not participating in how deep our roots tend to get.

According to Iowa State University Horticulture and Home pest news, it states, that roots will grow wherever the environment is favorable. They require water, oxygen, minerals, support and warmth. How many of us have been nurturing roots to expand in lifespan and grow deeper into our lives by not being proactive in uprooting them?

Just like a tree, if we aren't dismantling situations, aren't we clearly indirectly encouraging its behavior? Some may say, Nikkie, I hear you, I now see that I clearly haven't been dealing with my stuff, and have been attempting to cover it up, in hopes that it would just go away, however, that hasn't been working; so how do I get rid of this completely? Great question. Here's a simple 3-step process to start the journey, of uprooting, pulling up and diminishing this nuisance once and for all.

1. Identify your challenges- what is it that you are pretending not to know? It's clearly there but it's being masked by being busy with projects, work or with being a wife, mother, student, etc. Begin with the what you should bring awareness to and let's tackle it together. In order for us to even get to the next step, we have to go through a process of identification and labeling. Is this issue something that's blocking you? Is it keeping you from where you should be going in life? Is it hindering your relationships? What has this issue been keeping you from? We call this a limiting belief. This limiting belief paralyzes us mentally, emotionally and at times spiritually because we feel like what we are

taking in is truth and that's all we've been taught to do.

2. Whatever comes up for you, write it down–So many times, we don't get to experience our breakthrough because we forget to document the process. In this season, be mindful to keep your phone accessible, a recorder, notepad, pen and paper because you're the star of your own movie. When the blessings and miracles happen, you can recall how God brought you out.

3. Command that it changes – the word command normally has a negative connotation connected to it, and it can sound demanding, yet, according to dictionary. com it states that command means to give an authoritative order. Since we are all authority forces- Luke 10:19 says— "Look, I have given you authority over all the power of the enemy, and you can walk among snakes and scorpions and crush them. Nothing will injure you." With your words, you can command what you'd like to create in your life, relationships, career and repeat the process. The realization is to be aware that we should constantly affirm, speak into our life and make sure we are on guard with everything that's occurring.

We get to work through the temporary challenges of our lives all the while understanding that it's a temporary situation that we will get through as long as we are proactive in the process.

# Healing VS Fixing

There's a huge difference in taking the time to heal any wounds from your past and just suppressing them by putting a bandage on it; Hoping that this time, it will finally heal. Here's the glory behind the "level up." We can't take old habits into new seasons. What got you to where you are now, won't be the same mechanisms to take you to your next level. "To whom much is given, much is required."

If you've been blessed to be elevated and experience your territory being enlarged; and if you are able to activate a new level of consciousness, it's time to take a moment and apply some strategies that are designed for you to win. I remember a time when I would feel massive levels of stress from my business. Maybe a deal didn't come through or I was just overwhelmed with daily tasks. My initial thought was, let's grab a cocktail, or two and decompress. Having the cocktail for me, wasn't the challenge, it was my intent behind it.

I wanted to not feel what I was feeling, and I totally wanted to increase my endorphins aka my happy feelings. Listen, I just wanted to feel better for the moment. There's nothing wrong with having a cocktail either. In my case, I used it in an ineffective manner. In reality, I was stimulated by a substance that didn't serve me and I was using it for the wrong reasons. I was attempting to fix the stress, by becoming inebriated instead of healing the wound of imbalanced stress management.

Technically, I could've went to the gym and broke a sweat. Alcohol and exercise increase the same endorphins. In that moment, I realized that wisdom says, don't take old habits into new seasons. I am a new woman, with power, influence and love. I had to realize that there are better answers and I can access and implement new opportunities of growth. See, I had to understand how not to be married to the method. I had to divorce the desire and level up so I could come up.

Maybe this isn't a challenge for you. However, if you take a quick moment to self-evaluate, there may be an area in your life where you could be using an unhealthy method to substitute for a healthy new beginning. Here are a few ways to heal so you can move forward and conquer your next season in life.

1. Positive mental health is wealth- seeking professional help such as a therapist or counselor that can help you manage your emotional intelligence and keep you grounded in the right state of mind. Speaking to someone who can assist you with navigating how and what you're feeling can clear the path to a positive lifestyle and new beginning.

2. Exercising and training your body – raise your endorphins with me! Raising your awareness that exercise doesn't only make you look good but you also feel good as well. It does require discipline and a renewed mindset. With a minimum of 30 minutes of exercise a day, you can get the activity that you need and you can start feeling better. Change your mind, and in turn, you change your entire world. When we create an inner discipline within our minds, our bodies will follow.

3. Replace the _____ with _____ -think of some things you can replace your current habits with. This is the part where we retrain our brains to manifest what we currently want to see. We get to replace our current habits of overeating with healthy snacks and meals. We get to replace an over indulgence of drinking alcohol with exercising. This raises our feel-good

emotions called endorphins and allows us
to take better care of ourselves.

# 3 What's your way of being?

*"I AM creating a loving, vulnerable open and connected world."*

I've started to realize that my way of "being" is directly connected to how I'm showing up in life. When I am connected, loving, committed and giving, it shows and people are influenced to be the same way. I also invite others to consciously be aware of how they are showing up in life and with others.

The manner in which we are showing up, is manifesting in the lives of everyone we are connected to. It's sort of like we are enrolling others into a vision of how we want the world to respond. As for me, I've been attached to my way of "doing" for so long. What mattered to me was that I got stuff done. I am a master now at starting and finishing tasks. If you recall, from my first book Dreamers, Take Action!

I would never finish tasks. Everything I started,

I stopped before it even got a chance to hit the light of day. This time it's different. Practice makes perfect they say. Well, I say persistence manifests productivity. Keeping at it has helped me to build the momentum to execute at a high achievers level, whatever I put my hands on will be done and done in excellence. I quit playing games with myself and my gifts. This time around, the "doing" hasn't been the challenge. It's the "being."

In the process of being an influencer, a top brand and a voice to my community and the world at large, who was I really being when no one else was watching? Am I allowing my ego to step in and get in the way? Am I treating others how I would want to be treated? Or am I allowing this so-called acknowledgment to get to my everlasting head?

For the most part, I had to catch myself, when I'm not showing up in a way that effectively serves me or others. I have committed myself to show up consistently so that others have an example of how powerful it is to be present. Being present, and kind is what will really impact our communities and the world in a positive way.

It breaks my heart to hear about yet another mass shooting, robbery, suicide, rape or homicide. Who do we get to be collectively to eliminate devastating events? Who do we get to be for ourselves in order to see things change in our world? I make a public declaration for all women to step it up. The world needs powerful women who have the desire to remove weakness from their lives and their vocabulary. It's time for us to armor-up and stand for a world that's abundant, sustainable, loving, giving and understanding.

I saw a meme on Instagram once that said "In ancient Egyptian times, women were viewed and honored as the more sacred and valuable gender. They were held to a higher status than men. The woman is the nurturer and giver of all. She gives life and holds wisdom in her spirit as a powerful creative being. As men and women get together, the woman was expected to hold her man up. She gave him strength and prayed for his protection."

I'm not sure how accurate this meme was but it gave me chills. As the saying goes, "behind every successful man is a strong woman holding him up." Below, you'll find guidelines to being an IN-Powered woman. When we embody the IN-Powered lifestyle, we will then see the world become what we want. Only then, can we have a world that isn't desperate for a change, rather a world that together is so fruitful and joyful that it feels like heaven on earth.

Here are 10 guidelines to being an IN-Powered woman:

1. You can't be everything to everybody. But, you get to be everything for yourself. This is what truly makes you a Boss. I had to realize that I get to be alright with saying "no" in specific seasons of my life. As a leader and influencer, or even a woman in general, saying no often left me feeling guilty, or that I was disappointing others. But, there is a thin line between showing up and having a mental breakdown. Your mental health is a top priority. It's important to discern what season you're in and understand that you can't be everything to everyone.

2. Discern what's a fleshly desire or a spiritual necessity. Now we know when our flesh is rising up and looking for its quick fix. That's why we must know how to differentiate what's most important for the season that we are in. Also, making wise decisions on when your spirit man is on E and needs a quick fill up. Motivational videos, sermons and self-help books can assist with this.

3. IN-Powered women self-educate and don't self-medicate- You see this type of woman sees investing in her education as an art. We value, learning and growing. You may not have had a chance to attend a University or obtain a college degree, but there are a ton of ways that you can

invest in your education and professional development. There are certifications, licenses, programs, workshops, coaching, mentoring curriculums, courses, etc. that you can invest in to elevate yourself. I coach women who sometimes feel worthless because they don't have specific credentials to do more with their lives, however, it's never too late. Jim Rohn said it best when he said, "formal education will make you a living but self-education will make you a fortune."

4. An IN-Powered woman doesn't allow anyone to infiltrate her team- She is the Mama Bear of the community and always has an eye out for the best interest of her family and friends. She knows that prayer is the key ingredient to a winning life. She asks God to protect her surroundings, her possessions, the people she is invested in and her community. She keeps her home as a sacred space and asks God to keep her and her family. She has a winning life because she fully depends on God.

5. An IN-Powered woman focuses on her own home first- It's easy to take on a bunch of tasks and make such a strong attempt to fix the issues of everyone around you. It's easy to advise someone on how they should work through challenges in their

lives instead of stopping for a second and looking at what's not working in your own home. The word home could consist of our lives, our patterns and our mindsets. Some of my life coaching clients who happen to be women say to me that they are able to help everyone execute on their projects, visions and tasks and yet they are stuck with their projects and ideas, sitting on the backburner. Well, you know it's easier to snoop into others business and become Mrs. Fix-It while our homes are in shambles. Then we say, well, God what about me? Well, if you're too busy advancing everyone else and leaving yourself behind, then your life will continually be a birthing ground for miracles for someone else and never yourself. Take the spotlight off of others for a moment and put your focus on yourself and the gifts that God gave you and produce. Immediately.

6. We take the time to heal in the area of relationships. We get to spend time healing what hasn't been working in our relationships. That could be friendships, with our families, our spouses and even within ourselves. We see the significance of implementing ways to heal. This includes talking to a therapist, taking personal development workshops, spending time

with ourselves to learn who we are and making sure we are healed  before we try to heal others.

7. Don't forget the people who taught you and mentored you- I posted this mention in my Instagram stories, referencing that sometimes, you sow into, teach, mentor, coach or merely support some folks and they forget where they came from. It's disheartening when you've given to someone and you realize that they simply have taken elements of your brand, business or even life and try to redesign it and call it their own. Or you know that you've put in the work to help improve the life of someone else and it's like they have amnesia because they can't recall that you were the one who helped them get in position. Forgive anyway. The reality is that you won't always get a thank you or I appreciate you. Do good anyway. Be the one who chooses to get to sow into others without focusing on who is or isn't acknowledging you.

8. You can truly have it all, waiting for it to happen is a thing of the past – In the past, life has been an either-or conversation. I used to say, "I can only do this once, I have this." I had a hard time believing that life is abundant and wants to give to me daily.

Scarcity used to know my name. I want you to know that you get to enjoy all of life and its abundance and knowing that anything is possible. We get to stop operating from a scarcity mindset and open up to the possibilities of all that life has to offer.

9. Perfectionism is a thing of the past – The days are over for believing that every single action has to be perfect in order for it to be right. We are enough and no matter how much others have created unrealistic expectations for us, we get to design our lives and our destiny to reflect our own deep desires. Perfectionism doesn't exist and we get to dispel this idea in order to live the life we truly want.

10. Work-Life balance-Balance for me doesn't exist. Instead, priorities do. Seasons change and so do we. So, some things become important while others get placed on the back burner for a season. What are the top 5 important elements of your life currently? For me, my top 5 are God, my gifts, myself, my relationships and some fun. I get to implement fun into my life on a daily basis. Consider your top 5 and keep those priorities in the front and center. All other elements will get in where they fit in. I think about when we were in school and our teachers would ask, what would

you like to be when you grow up? Instead of saying a doctor, a lawyer, a teacher, or a news reporter, instead, we could respond to I'd like to be loving, compassionate, giving, caring and supportive. See, this is a world that creates children who will one day become adults in a generation that sees and believes in themselves and others.

# THE IN-POWERED WOMAN

# 4 Healing is on the other side of Trauma and abuse

*"I AM experiencing total health in all areas of my life."*

My greatest moments of trauma have produced my most profound pieces of work. It's as if life has taken me on a roller-coaster of endless emotions that takes me up one day and completely down the next.

You may have seen a smile, but I was feeling heartbreak. You've seen affirmation, but I've suffered with battles in my mind where my thoughts traveled at a million miles a minute. I had to remind myself to stay present. What are you feeling in this exact moment? How are you embracing this exact moment in time that will be the deciding factor to catapult you to your place of completion?

Society calls what I am experiencing right now,

feelings. Me? I call it, reality. Research shows that our minds, as brilliant and remarkable as they are, process thoughts at some 80,0000 thoughts a day, 80% are negative and 90% are repetitive from the day before.

Seriously? How do I even maintain myself on a daily basis with a mindset like that? Feels like I'm in a time capsule, traveling back into time, into space, looking for an answer, a whisper, some guidance, just anything.

I am a creative. My mind is colorful, stupendous, sometimes out of this world. I can't get a grip on myself, if I allowed it. Even if I wanted to, I probably wouldn't. My mind tells me so many things. Half of the time, I opened my mouth and contradict the very thing I am thinking. When I feel overwhelmed, I create. When I feel restless, overworked, exhausted, or despair, I create. It reaffirms that I don't have to waste anything.

All of the energy that funnels through my body has to go somewhere, or it will lie dormant or even manifest in other ways. That could be through illness or through sickness. However, I chose to allow it to go into the form of creation. In the good book, it says that all things are working for my good. Well, if that's the case, even in the moment, of massive heartbreak, I can prevail and reign triumphant in my journey of life.

I feel like I've lost as much as I've gained. I feel as if God makes each moment up to me and sort of reimburses me when I endure the pain. What's next for me? I can't release this work, it's so vulnerable, personal, and even intimate. It feels like I'm putting my heart out on a sheet of paper for the world to examine, pick apart, and explore. The expectation for greatness feels like a slippery slope.

So, I chose to do this my way. Clearly, I can't take another second of disappointment. So, I talk myself through the process. You'd hear me speak clearly, with words that would paint the canvas of the most talented artist known to man. I'd say things like "it is well, it's working out, stay present, keep focused on your life & goals, don't get caught up."

I've had a barricade up to block out anyone who wants to love me, clearly there's trust issues there. Listen, if you experienced even half of my life, you would probably be the same way. Guarded, scared, afraid, wanting love but simply you're convinced if you do, you're bound to be hurt.

Then I tell myself, it's about being brave, can you be brave? I had to learn to be alone for a bit. My entire life, I had plans to be married by 25, have children with my dream guy and live near the ocean, where we could see the seagulls flying throughout the sky as the sun shined effortlessly.

I imagined my children being intelligent, witty, fun, extra and wonderful, just wonderful. My husband, 6 ft 3 in tall, slender in build, yet athletic; sensitive but a manly man, loving, heartfelt, thoughtful, mighty, victorious and a warrior. A man that would bless me with the gift of children. I visualized my family and I felt so much internal joy and a refreshing that reminded me that this was real and so possible for me. Now, as I sit here and write this, I am now 32, single and currently childless.

The hurt that transpires throughout my body, reminds me that we don't always get what we want when we want it. I think about my time in college, when I got the wish to be a mother. I was 5 months pregnant when I had an abortion.

I was misguided, unsure and clearly, didn't know what I was doing. I messed up and that regret weighed me down for 5 years, until one day I finally forgave myself. All the should've, could've would've filled my mind. But, I made the choice, I didn't know what I was doing. I didn't have a mentor, or coach or someone to just show me that there was a better way.

So, my heart goes out to young women who feel like a baby would ruin their lives. That was my mindset, but I wish I chose different at the time.

I don't stand here in condemnation because I know the Lord forgave me and I forgave myself as well. But, the thought still comes to my mind and reminds me that my life would've been different had I just said yes. Had I surrendered to the possibility of being a mother. Though the mechanism was different, the gift was still sealed with a gentle kiss. You see, I had plans for my life.

I drafted every step out on a blueprint guide as if an architect created this vision. I was the creator with pen and paper in hand. However, it still hasn't happened. Is it me? Are my standards absurd and unreachable? Has this generation gone mad? Are there any phenomenal men left, or must I just settle for the first man that catches my attention? No, settling. I now see how blocked I've been from love.

I had the desire, however, I didn't realize I was standing in my own way of breakthrough. I was removing myself from the possibility of having a phenomenal life. Oh, now I remember. The block came from my first encounter of being sexually assaulted. From a guy whom I trusted. I had started dating him a week after my mother passed away from cancer.

He was a sound voice and honestly, someone who I just needed for some sort of comfort during that time. Not only that, he was friends with one of my family members, so I was safe, right? Wrong. My own flesh and blood made a comment to me about not bringing this information to her attention sooner, and her final response?

"I'm glad you told me but I'm not going to stop being his friend." My heart shattered because I wasn't expecting her to respond in that way. Why would she say that? The sense of love, connection and compassion was non-existent and in that moment I knew our relationship would never be the same.

I would love her, but I would do so from a distance and I am alright with that. My advice is that when you're grieving, depending on what you can handle, maybe dating isn't the best option. Honestly, be open to receiving love from friends and family members that you trust. Putting trust into the hands of someone whom you just met may put you and your life in a compromising position. The entire ordeal put me in a position to not ever trust men again. No wonder I couldn't be in love with a man, I didn't trust them.

The one that I believed wouldn't take advantage of me, did and never in a million years would I have believed that this could happen to me. I'm a strong and powerful woman. However, in a moment of despair, I was caught where my guards were down, I was vulnerable and that person saw an opportunity and he took it.

I want you to know that the story or situation doesn't stop there. For many women who can relate to this, my hat goes off to you for being open to speak up about the occurrence. According to Rainn.org, 1 out of every 6 American women have been the victim of an attempted or completed rape in her lifetime (14.8% completed, 2.8% attempted) this doesn't even show justice for the countless women globally who are sexually assaulted around the world. According to world population review, 35% percent of women worldwide have experienced some sort of sexual assault in their lifetime.

Less than 40% of women seek out help. With such alarmingly high statistics, we get to do something about this for ourselves and for each other. First, I want you to know that what happened to you is not your fault. It happened, yes, but you are not to blame. We get to use this situation as a way to know that we can and will get through to a more powerful side of the story.

We are authoring this very moment and it's up to us to rewrite the narrative. As women, we get to navigate ourselves out of compromising situations. Sometimes, we may not even know something could happen to us. For me, I didn't even know what I was experiencing because this has never happened to me before.

However, we get to just be aware of our surroundings. If you know something feels off while you're around someone, please ask for a friend to be present or to lend a helping hand for you to get out of the situation. Always, let your family or friends know where you are going. Send them your location or an address to where you are with the person you are with. Sometimes, there isn't a cookie cutter way to prevent this or any violating situation from happening however, we can be proactive in our healing process.

For me therapy has helped me to identify and call the situation what it was, but also to work through my healing through awareness, self-love, compassion, and activities that have assisted with even being able to speak up on this. There's not one way to do this, and for each person I believe there's a new or different way.

My recommendation would be therapy or speaking to a trusted professional that can help you walk through this. I also participated in a personal development training called gratitude training. This training has 3 components to it. Part 1. Discovery this part of the training helps you discover any blocks that you may be facing. Self-limited beliefs that have you stuck in a box and not allowing you to live the life of your dreams.

Part 2. Breakthrough-oh, my! This is the bread and butter. You know all of those discoveries you came across in part 1? You now get to breakthrough all of them and receive support and love from your entire community, team and now family. Part 3. Masterful Living, it's your life. If you really want the life that you've always dreamed of, this training will show you how and open up so much for you in the process. After I went on this journey of personal development, it opened up so much for me and helped me identify what wasn't working in my life and what was.

Once I went through this process, my entire life started to glow from the inside out. It helped me to start creating the life that I always said I wanted. It opened up a new relationship for me, I became a certified transformational life coach and it also helped me launch my life coaching agency.

I started saying yes to my life and a new start. I stopped resisting, and gave myself the opportunity to receive all that I said I wanted to have in my life. I am grateful for this new start and being honest about my healing has been a true gem for me. I realize that when we are open and we surrender to the process in life, we then create breakthroughs and miracles in our lives and the lives of others.

So, what can you proactively apply into your life now? Maybe your story isn't like mine. Maybe you've experienced some other type of trauma or grief. How do you get to manifest your healing from this situation?

You owe it to yourself to remove the blocks so you can start living the life you truly desire. You don't know what you don't know if you don't know it. My honest advice is to seek out help. Don't allow whatever you've gone through to keep you in a box. Heal my sister. It feels great to be on the other side. Victory is for you and with you. Grab it, embrace it and allow it to take you to where you want to be on this journey in life.

# 5

## Are you Winning from Within?

*"I AM designing my greatest life, starting from within me first."*

I sit here and wonder when was the first time, I accepted the fact that settling was normal. When I allowed mediocrity to become my new normal. Why did I settle?

Why did I allow the men who came into my life, asking me to be with them give me subpar relationships? Why when I saw red flag after red flag, did I decide to turn the other cheek and make excuses for behavior that I knew did not represent my worth. I would say something like, "oh, Nikkie, it's not that serious." This is a behavior that can be worked on. He didn't mean it.

Maybe if you pray, God will just change him and then you could move on and become a celebrated power couple?

We would take perfectly lit pictures, with the famous #RelationshipGoals hashtag. We would steal the internet and be approved by the Instagram critics. When did I become so desperate that I allowed myself to sink into allowing men to treat me like I wasn't enough, worthy or valuable?

Living our lives based off of societal norms, puts us in the position to have to bend to what others believe we should be or have. What am I talking about here? Well, relationships with men, wasn't always my strong suit.

I take accountability for how I've become so intertwined with wanting this fairytale lifestyle that I allowed men who I wouldn't have in a million years, date me. When I tell you, these have been the time wasters, non-committed, focused on the wrong thing, type of men. Did I have a challenge with attracting successful men? Nope, that wasn't it. Was there integrity and character in position? To say the least, nope.

How did I start attracting this type of man? In reality? What was I pretending not to know? Well, my breaking point was after I dated a guy who had three children with three different women. He was fun and loved taking me out. He wined and dined me but I knew good and well, I would never allow this man to wed me. We should all have non-negotiables and one of mine was, I don't date men with children, much less, three with three different women involved.

This sounds even worse, hearing myself describe this. I totally believe it's a beautiful thing to see men take care of their children, however, for me, I want my first child to be with the man I marry. See, that's the thing.

Why did I bend on my non-negotiables? I've learned that when you settle for what you really don't want into your life, you allow yourself to miss out on all the beautiful memories you could create with the person who is really for you. However, someone is sitting on the throne of your heart, taking up space.

While the real King is waiting to be take his royal position. I get it. Sometimes, as you're on your journey, it gets a bit cold, sometimes, lonely and you're ready to be wifed up and swept off of your feet. Society, says it's about time, but, if it's not your true heart's desire, just wait your turn. Hold out, keep praying and asking God for strength on this journey.

Is it easier said than done? Absolutely. But you have to be convinced that your time will come. It reminds me in the scripture of Abraham who by faith believed and hoped that he would become the Father of many nations. God told him that's how many descendants he would have.

Abraham was 100 years old, yet still his faith didn't waver. This is why God counted him as righteous. In all actuality, his faith grew stronger because he believed—Romans 4:18-22. Now, let me tell you this, I had to dig deeper within myself to figure out what impacted my ability to create the choices that I was creating. If you have been mistreated, betrayed, abused or emotionally neglected in a relationship, sometimes, it makes sense to take a step back and realize what's manifesting. Whether in a relationship or friendship, in your selection process, it would be of service to you to select your spouse or friend with wisdom.

The Bible says, those who are wise will shine like the brightness of the heavens, Daniel 12:3. My go-to is to be with someone who embodies the love and heart of Christ. It's something about the love of Christ that exudes through someone as the brightest light in the middle of the ocean beaming down from a light tower. The tangible expression of God's love feels like a baby who kisses you on the cheek when you need a pick-me upper.

Sitting in a room and feeling a strong, yet gentle presence overtake you while you bask in the moment of an overwhelming and loving spirit. What a joy to be loved this way. Also, to mention God finds great pleasure in blessing our lives, families, finances, businesses and relationships. When you're with a person who carries the heart of God inside of them, you'll find a spirit that encompasses safety, nurture, generosity, acceptance and comfort.

These are winning attributes that keep on giving. When you're in the vetting process of who to date, befriend or even marry, ask yourself, does this person carry the love of God? It's alright for a person to just be on the journey to knowing God or maybe they haven't reached the revelation about who God is yet and you can support them with that. The selection process sort of looks like remembering what you deserve. Who do you want to be with? What are their values? What are their ways of being? How do they show up in the world?

Are they loving, supportive, giving and committed to you? Are they treating you as the Queen that you are? Well, why not because you do deserve it and you must always tell yourself that. I've noticed that when it comes to selecting your future spouse, there must be a level of awareness of God in them.

I also would say go as far as them having a personal relationship with God. And if you're a believer just the way I am then, also knowing Jesus as their savior. Now, I'm not referring to religion. I'm speaking of them having their own prayer life, their own love language and own personal connection with Jesus.

Because when stuff hits the fan, you need someone

who can show up for you in a way that will help you through the situation. Someone to pray for you. You also want to be with a person who is so connected to your breakthrough that they will stand as a source of compassion, love and support. It's a powerful way to create an impact within your own life. An IN-Powered woman understands that the people in her life raises her up. They shift her to a level of thinking and they help her become more of her higher self each and every day.

They call her out on her stuff, and they also show her how she can improve. All in all, it's done out of love. When God is in the midst of that equation; two powerful beings can design the best life with endless possibilities.

I sat back and thought about my relationships, and why in the past it probably didn't work for me. Maybe, it stemmed from the relationship with my Father. You know they say, whatever happened in your relationship with your parents as a child can reflect in your current relationships as an adult, if you let it. Well, I didn't have that challenge. My Dad and I grew up inseparable. Two peas in a pod.

I played the role of a good child. You know, go to school, get good grades, be the captain of the dance team, show up for my yearbook photos, all of the above. Except I actually used to skip school, I forged my report card to pretend my grades were excellent and had to go to an adult vocational school to make up my grades so I could graduate high school. Oh, don't forget sneaking out the house to hang out with my adult boyfriend who was 6 years my senior. You see, I was pretending to be perfect. My Dad had me on a high pedestal that there's no way I could live up to his high expectations. This wasn't his fault though.

My Dad was an excellent parent and he took care of his four children the best way he knew how and when he didn't, he gave us over to God to help him make the best choices that he could. I didn't want to disappoint my Dad ever, I wanted to make my father proud and I wanted the beautiful gifts and the cars, clothes, so I pretended to "be" someone I was not and couldn't be even though I tried. So, I got use to wearing this mask to please people.

If you couldn't see the real me, then you would love me, take care of me and buy me things. It was a form of manipulation that I had absolutely no idea, I was taking part in. Now, this didn't make me a bad person, but it did teach me how to put on and wear my first mask called "inauthentic". After finishing high school, I told myself, I had to get out of my city.

There was nothing there after high school for

me. All of my friends went away to school and I was left there trying to figure out what was next. If I didn't take so much time faking it, I probably could've gotten into the college I wanted to be at which at the time was Clark Atlanta. However, due to my grades, I didn't get accepted, I was bummed and disappointed.

I applied to an HBCU, and by the grace of God and prayer, I got accepted into FAMU. When I was first heading out to college, I remember sitting in the living room and I saw my Daddy pacing back and forth in the living room. My Daddy looked at me and said, you're going to college, and "I am betting my money on you. Go to school and do what you're supposed to do."

That was a lot of pressure. I really just wanted to show my Daddy that I could be perfect. I could finally get myself together and allow my Daddy to be happy and satisfied with my work. Not with who I was. As I share this, I am choosing to take full accountability for my actions. It was never his fault. In fact, the way my Dad showed up in my life helped me to be a greater woman today. So, many times, we try to blame our parents, family or friends for how our lives are turning out. So, not cool.

We are authoring and curating every single moment of our lives. We are doing it, with our powerful selves. So, instead of trying to relive the unrealistic expectations of others, how about we live our lives for ourselves.

As an IN-Powered woman, no matter the situation, we take ownership for designing our future and destiny. We don't even get to blame God for how our lives turn out. "Woe, is me, little ol' me, my life is a mess." No, we get to operate in the mindset of "faith without works is dead." You see Faith and works are the winning combination. I meet so many women who say, "I have the faith and I'm waiting on God." Well, my dear you'll be waiting until kingdom comes, because God nor the universe operates in that way.

You get to be a powerful IN-Powered woman and say whatever I have the faith for will manifest once I activate my superpower which is doing my part, by doing the work. Work is your activation in the earth. When you apply your hands to create something positive in the world, God, the Angels, the universe and everything around you conspire against your opposition to make it happen for you.

I remember one client that came through my life coaching program, sought out my services for 90 days and she needed to get refocused on her business. She had so many great ideas but couldn't seem to get a grip on what was happening and how to manifest anything she wanted to do. I mean, of course, she had so much going on that her focus was off and she lacked clarity to create. As her life coach, I helped her see endless possibilities to become a successful entrepreneur.

I helped her create strategies and it was an amazing feeling to see her apply the strategies and get the results that she's been attempting to get in the last 6 years. Seeing it manifest within less than 90 days for was so rewarding for me. That's the greatest gift my clients can give me is their ability to do the work (faith) and apply the action (works) their winning ingredient is having me as their life coach and accountability partner to take them to the next level. My client asked me a question, she said, "how do you keep such faith while you're in the process? My challenge is that sometimes I don't even believe it can happen for me." I acknowledged her for sharing with me, and allowing me to walk her though what a breakthrough could be for her.

I told her, I myself have days where I don't feel like it's possible or can happen. Or I even doubt my ability to create. That's natural because I am human and when those moments happen I send out gratitude to God and the universe for sending me the nudges that remind me that I'm not a robot who doesn't feel, I have the same emotions as everyone else if not more intense, however I am so determined to make it happen that it will and it must.

One thing I won't do is quit on my commitments and promises to myself. I vow to complete whatever it is that I said I would do. So, my faith may be a little shaky sometimes, however, I remember that my commitments to myself outweigh any fear, discouragement, worry or self-doubt.

I go back to the scripture that says if I have faith as small as a mustard seed, I can do and be anything. She understood this so clearly and in that moment, we made such a connection with each other that she saw me in a way that brought us together. She realized that though I was her life coach, I was still a woman who is on the same journey as she is.

IN-Powered women know that they too can become all that they want to be if they only believe. If there is ever a moment when their faith becomes shaky, they understand that they have backup to support them through it all. What an amazing feeling to have this available to us.

# THE IN-POWERED WOMAN

# 6 The Law of Act & Attract

*"I AM attracting what I want into my life."*

You have just entered into a space that will take your mind into a whole new dimension if you allow it. There are universal laws that if you apply these laws, the exact desires that you truly want to experience will be manifested into your life.

You see, here's the thing, manifestation is a tool that we all have access to. We can literally, speak a thing and watch it happen right before our eyes. Now, there are other times where a process occurs, but we will touch on that later.

You see, this chapter is beyond manifestation and attraction. If that's what you're looking for, you can tap into the law of attraction for that. What I speak of here, is an opportunity to apply scriptural laws, follow a set of practical steps and also have a team of support and security in this stage of creation. Before we tap into anything, the first thing we most focus on is identity. I must do my due diligence by informing you about who you are. Once you know this, manifestation at high levels will be effortless for you. Isn't that what you want?

The ability to create any level of happiness and fulfillment at the cost of your own declarations? This sounds magical. Well, it's not magic at all, it's also not some mumbo jumbo hocus pocus remedy. What I speak of, is undeniable and indisputable creation directly from the mouth of God. Want to know what else this isn't? It's not religion, no offense to anyone who practices religion, this book just isn't based on religious principles, rather, relationship.

It's the ability to ignite within you, the power that you already have. The only challenge is this "power" we speak of, has been untapped, bound and maybe even undeveloped.

In this chapter, we will develop an identity that places you in the position of royalty. Your inheritance will be unlocked and discovered. What I am truly excited the most about is how powerful you will be after reading this. I only ask of one favor. That if you're making the choice to go on this journey, you're 100% open to receive what you'll learn here.

That you will demystify all mindsets that can

block you from abundantly walking into your victory. I want to explore a life with you that I've been exposed to. Now, if you've read my book Dreamers, Take Action! You will see this chapter is as an extension of that. Yes, DTA was a blueprint for taking action, however this my friend is a rewrite of everything that we were taught about manifesting the life we truly desire.

I believe that we were all designed to create. Apart of our identity is that we are co-creators to Christ. The interesting part is that someone reading this may feel as if they aren't a believer in God. Well, let me be clear before we move forward. Whether you are agnostic, atheist, or practice other religious principles that says that Jesus isn't the son of God, I want to say I understand and this chapter still applies to you as well.

What I am teaching here has more to do with your power through God and scripture. What I would charge you to do is, give yourself a shot at simply reading this information and applying it regardless of your beliefs. What we aren't doing here is forcing any spiritual principles upon you but offering you an opportunity to accessing your birthright. We are teaching you how to tap into your generational bloodline for explosive blessings.

I would challenge you to study this information

and try it. Now, is this information for everyone? Absolutely not, however, I wouldn't dismiss the fact that an opportunity to create your best life now through your own personal power is ready and available for you to arrive and access it. So, give it a shot. Read and study this book in its entirety. Once, you've finished practice what you've read. These are proven laws that will change the trajectory of your life if you allow it to.

The best part of this book is that you don't have to sell your soul to have this type of power. As an IN-Powered woman you get to use your words to manifest your life as you put in the work to create it. John 1:1 says "in the beginning was the Word, and the Word was with God, and the Word was God." For me, this means that the word of God manifests into a tangible expression once it's spoken.

This proves that we are clearly attracting our lives into existence by what we are saying. As we speak, IN-Powered women, know that as divine ultimate creatures, we are constantly creating. So think through what you're speaking into your world before you open your mouth and speak it over your life or the lives of others.

Here are some scriptures below that can help give you knowledge on the power that you currently have. Read these scriptures, meditate on them, recite them and own them. They will be a great start to you tapping into your natural born power and presence.

**Philippians 4:13**—I can do all things through Christ who gives me strength.

**Isaiah 40:29**—He gives strength to the weary and increases the power of the weak.

**Deuteronomy 8:18**—Remember the Lord your God. He is the one who gives you power to be successful.

**Habakkuk 3:19**—The Sovereign Lord is my strength; he makes my feet like the feet of deer, he enables me to tread on the heights.

**Ephesians 3:16**—I pray that out of his glorious riches he may strengthen you with his power through his Spirit in your inner being.

**Luke 10:19**—Look, I have given you authority over all the power of the enemy, and you can walk among snakes and scorpions and crush them. Nothing will injure you.

**Joel 3:10**—Let the weakling say that I AM Strong!

Start with these scriptures, get them down into your spirit and start owning your true identity to attract exactly what you want into your life through taking action!

# 7

## You're the bag! Secure yourself

*"I AM putting myself in the position to win-BIG!"*

We have heard the coined term "secure the bag." The term has a few definitions to it. One can mean to make your money, another can mean to take hold of a situation, take advantage of it from a positive aspect and keep it sacred and valuable. In this case, I want to reference keeping something of value (yourself) and taking advantage of every positive and life-changing situation that may be presented to you.

One way to secure the bag for yourself is to work on your mind. Your mind is so powerful and honestly, each second of the day you're authoring your life through your thoughts and words.

I can't even begin to explain how much your life is being called into existence by what you're saying. Let me begin by sharing how much affirmations can transform your life if you allow it. I went through stages and seasons of my life where I affirmed myself so much that I started to believe everything I was speaking.

I was rewiring my subconscious and pouring positivity into my mind to create a ripple effect of newness in my life. I was literally attracting everything that I was speaking daily. So, I figured if I was negative, I would be attracting all types of unwanted vibes into my space. No, Bueno! I'll pass. There was a time, in my office building, when I had my mentee come and add sticky notes with affirmations on my door.

Each morning people would take the affirmations and add them to their office desks, their doors, in their wallets and they would say to me, "wow, this really helped me or thank you for spreading positivity in our office."

It was such a powerful whirlwind of change that people started gravitating to my office asking me to be their life coach. I couldn't believe what we had manifested with a simple act of discernment and obedience.

People need affirmations and it truly changes the way we see ourselves. Now don't get me wrong, as scripture says, Faith without works is dead as we spoke about previously. So, this means you get to put action behind your words. Yes, affirmations are rewriting all negative narratives however, when we do the work, we get to see how much our lives are being positioned for the blessings that God has for us. I speak positivity because I know as an IN-Powered woman, every second I am creating and generating the results to my life and I matter.

As an IN-Powered woman you get to be mindful of what you're saying about yourself and to others. Let me start you off with your first set of affirmations on abundance. This is a quick start to speaking positivity into your atmosphere so you can experience the life that you desire and want to see manifest for you.

This entire audio playlist of themed affirmations are available on YouTube under the name Affirm by Nikkie Pryce, so take a listen to it when you can. Feel free to download the playlist and write out these affirmations on sticky notes or simply rewrite and print this sheet so you can hang them up on your wall, in your office, in your home or any visible space where you can see the affirmations.

# Abundance Affirmations

1. Only good can come to me.

2. What I AM seeking is seeking me.

3. I AM financially abundant and everything I need is within me.

4. I unlock the prosperity that is within me.

5. I remove any limitation, scarcity mindset and lack from within my life.

6. I AM fulfilled and satisfied with my abundant and successful life.

7. Success follows me and I welcome it into my life.

8. I AM over sufficient, I have more than enough and I get to give some away.

9. I AM the lender, never the borrower.

10. I AM financially successful, I manage my abundant money well.

11. I AM always overflowing in the more than enough.

12. I always have more than I can imagine.

13. I AM favored by God, and favor runs and chases me down.

14. People go out of their way to be good to me.

15. I can be whatever, do whatever and have whatever.

16. There are no limitations for me. I have every single thing I need in my abundant life.

17. I am so full of abundance and I have way more than I can manage.

18. People connected to me are blessed by my abundance.

19. I love being abundant and overflowing in prosperity.

20. Abundance is my birthright and I deserve it in my life.

21. I ALWAYS have enough in my life.

22. I am abundant in every area of my life.

23. My spiritual, emotional, mental, physical and financial are all overflowing in greatness.

Affirmations help us speak positive outcomes into existence.

# THE IN-POWERED WOMAN

# 8 Relationship Validation

*"I AM willing to learn and grow from others"*

Many IN-Powered women know how to get the job done. Let's be honest, with how skillful and talented we are, if you give us the opportunity, we can manage any task you put before us. Getting the job done is a cinch, and if we are asked to make it happen, trust me it will get done.

The word, lazy is non-existent in our vocabulary. That's amazing to know, however, how are you being while you're doing? Yes, what you're doing is awesome, but when someone asks you to do something, do you feel the blood raise in your body and the thought "I despise being told what to do" come across your mind?"

Who do they think they are anyway, telling me what to do? The ego rises to the occasion and sets in to say, "I am my own boss, I get to call the shots. Who do they think they are talking to?"

One of my mentors is an investment banker. He's loaded with wisdom in life & with numbers and in turn, he's loaded in his pockets as well. When I'm privileged to get a chance to sit with him in his office, I'm completely humbled and all I do is listen. When I'm there, I have nothing to say.

My job is to listen to the nuggets that he drops in to my ear. He's sharing with me the keys to success. He says things like "Nikkie, write everything down, every single goal, every single thought, write it down and when you accomplish it scratch it off the list."

When I'm amongst him and other millionaires, I humble myself and take it all in. Why you say? Aren't I someone who should have an opinion or a voice? Well, of course I do, however, I share when I absolutely know it's needed. If not, I'm listening. I'm listening because I want to be on the end of the table where they are sitting.

They've already paid their dues and I am more interested in learning what they did right vs. walking into the room with them as if I know it all.

When we think we know it all and aren't open to being taught new things and aren't willing to be coachable, we shut down all possibilities to be increased in our lives. Being in the room with millionaires, the conversation is different. Even the energy in the room is different. They are discussing big money moves and not concerned with matters that don't matter in the first place.

Honestly, it's not just about the money talk that intrigues me. It's the fact that the same people who have the same 24 hours as me, are growing and scaling at such a magnetic frequency that I am convinced that the same can happen for me, and for you too.

So, my way of being while I'm in the company of millionaires? I am being humble, attentive, focused and connected. This isn't the time to give off an attitude that says "I don't need to listen to what you have to say or do what you say to do." Now is the time to be grateful that I get to be in the room and focus on receiving. I shared this message with one of my clients who is enrolled into my 90-day empowerment life coaching program.

We discussed her working for me for a semester while she sat out of college. When I would request of her to get something done, she would absolutely get the job done, however, she would give off an energy like she didn't want to listen or take direction from me.

We sat and talked about this. I asked her a series

of questions which led up to, "are you getting the results that you truly want from life?" She said no. I asked her how does she play "team" with others? She stated that she didn't like taking orders from others. I simply told her, there are certain results you want to see in your life and how you BE while you DO is really making all the difference.

Playing "team" instead of seeing this as a one-person show can create a ripple effect of support that can take your career to the next level and let's be honest, the world doesn't need another woman with an "attitude problem." We need powerful women who are willing to learn, play team and grow, so that we can all get to the next level together.

So, the next time that it's asked of you to play team with your sister, whether that woman looks like you or not, remember how much more we get to accomplish together. Remember how the world can be a better place once women start standing in their position and showing up for each other.

Remember that this isn't a Black, White, Asian, Hispanic, etc. conversation, this is how can I support the vision of another woman so we can all take ourselves to the next level. Even if you already know the answer to something, would it kill you to listen? Maybe you'll learn something new from the conversation.

We are always students at life, gleaning from the conversations of others. We don't need to be in competition with each other. Let's stop putting ourselves against each other, because as we see, that's not taking us anywhere.

Let's humble ourselves and listen to what we can learn to create the life that we truly want and let's also start being loving, attentive, focused and kind while we get the job done. Let's create a world that sees and knows that when we support each other and choose to play team, then people know that they matter. We are validated by ourselves.

Our approval happens when we see ourselves as worthy and valuable. When we stand in our rightful positions and make powerful requests to ourselves to step it up and become all that we need to be to make the world a better place. You see, so many times, I've coached women who felt like they had a point to prove. That others should recognize their greatness. That they would be the voice that's heard instead of trampled all upon. That they felt if they raised their voice, yelled a little louder, waved their hands in the air, that someone somewhere would finally listen to them.

However, it's presence that needs to show up

first. A secure woman doesn't need to make a whole heap of noise to be seen or even heard. Her presence shows a great impact and people recognize her. People want to be around women who know their value and worth. Self-value isn't arrogance it's charismatic. The lack of self-value is arrogance and disrespectful to our creator.

# How to Navigate in a Male Dominated Industry

Ok, so as an IN-Powered woman it is important to know how to maneuver in an environment that may not at times support your endeavors. Now, don't get me wrong, I know a ton of men who support women, love us, encourage our endeavors and help us to move forward in our lives. They are the peach to our cobbler. They see us, love us, connect with us and have our backs.

I want to personally send a special thank you to men worldwide who love us and keep us safe. This space is to just remind IN-Powered women how to hold their own in male dominated spaces with grace and ease. I remember when I worked in corporate America. I worked primarily with men, on top of that I was the only young black woman in this specific environment amongst two other caucasian women and five men.

At times, it felt like a power trip. Who can do what better than who? It felt like the women were put against the men, to sell more products, connect more and to make more money than the men in our store. However, when we compared the numbers, the men made a significantly higher salary over all the women there. So, I had to learn quickly how to maneuver in an environment that may not have been setup for me to win.

I'll drop 3 top insightful tips to help you remember how to conquer in a male dominated industry and still keep your composure, integrity, heart and commitment to creating a world that's positive and loving.

1. Know that what's for you is for you-You don't need to beg, scratch, scream or yell for your position. What's for you will appear before you as you prepare for its arrival. I stand by the phrase, when the student is ready the teacher appears. Even in an environment that's pumped by testosterone, you can still have what's for you as long as you do your part and do your work.

2. Know your business and mind it-In order to win and win big in any industry, you must know your stuff. There's no way, you can put yourself in position if you haven't

taken the time to self-educate yourself. Take time to read material and books to take your knowledge to the next level. Take courses, workshops or trainings that teach what you need to know in your industry. No one should have to give you the information that you haven't taken the time to learn. There is nothing like a woman who is on her job and knows her stuff.

3. Create Allies - AKA teammates. No one woman is an island. In order to do great work, you must have others in position so that you can focus on your most important tasks. Work with others, even the men on your team and learn from them. So much more can be created if we can work together. Acts 6 in the bible discusses how the apostles put wise and faith driven men in position so that they could focus on learning and teaching the gospel. Be like the Apostles. Engage with trusted teammates and create more together than apart.

# 9

# Success Attracts Success

*"I AM A successful woman who attracts successful people and opportunities."*

There was a point in my life that I had to realize that I was successful.

I had to understand that the opportunities and open doors that started to fly open for me, I had attracted into my life. I realized that the Grace and Favor from God embraced me with a scented aroma that catapulted me before great men and women. The Bible says that your gift will make room for you and bring you before great men – Proverbs 18:16. I had to realize that success was my portion.

Earlier on when I first launched my business, I walked around with the idea that I wasn't good enough. That I didn't drive the car as my colleagues or live in the big expensive house yet, and I used that idea to validate my success.

When I realized the lives that I transformed through my life coaching, speaking and workshops, I began to redefine what success means to me. You see, one term according to dictionary.com means the accomplishment of one's goals. I agree with this statement 100%.

Why you ask? Because success to me truly means, creating a world that has been impacted and inspired by my presence. I have come to the realization that people are always watching us. They are watching and waiting for us to show up, to do our best and do our part. In reality, people want to be around other people who are winning. People want to be seen with winners.

The ones who are making the most change in their communities, churches, on their teams, in their organizations and frankly, in the world. No one wants to be with someone who is busy complaining, nagging, always discussing others and what they don't want in their lives. Success breeds success. I attended a successful networking event on South Beach, Miami. The room was filled with successful people who were making moves and connecting themselves with other people who were making major moves.

You see when you're in a room like that, the conversations are different. As an IN-Powered woman, you want to be around other successful women who can assist you as you navigate towards your next level. Think of what you want to accomplish in the next days, weeks, months and years. Then strap up those designer pumps and get to moving.

A millionaire told me once, that he writes down every single goal he wants to accomplish daily. This is truly so helpful because you can physically visualize what needs to get done and apply it.

# THE IN-POWERED WOMAN

# 10

## We get to Play T.E.A.M

*"I AM an IN-Powered woman who knows she never has to travel this road alone."*

Team. Together everyone achieves more. I used to always feel like I wasn't supported. I used to tell myself, get it done on your own. If people want to help me, and support me then they would just show up and I wouldn't have to ask. What a weird way to live.

What an unfortunate attitude to have. When we play team, we end up being able to lean on each other for support, encouragement, love and connection. When two or more are gathered together, God will be in the midst of a situation. That simply means that doing life alone, will put such a damper on your energy, your mind and spirit. This morning as I woke up, I prayed and asked God for a strategy to execute effectively in my day.

As I referenced earlier, Acts 6 discusses the Apostles wanting to stay in their position to teaching the word of God instead of running a food program. It wasn't that the position wasn't significant, however, they needed to focus on what their calling and position was.

They built a team so others could serve in the capacity where they needed help. They understood the value of team and putting others in position. I have learned the value of this in my own life. My greatest challenge has been to ask for help or support. My ego stood in the way of making genuine connections and receiving love from others.

When I took a stand, and told myself that it's ok to get help, it's ok to network and meet other women and it's ok to know that I'm never ever competing with my sister. I am only completing the task that's before me. Just as the Apostles did. As an IN-Powered woman we understand that friendships lead to prosperity and favor in our lives.

There are people assigned to our destinies to help us get to the next level. And if we allow our egos to get in the way, we miss out on our acceleration of next level promotion. My advice, learn to work with others and learn it quick. You're one person away from your next breakthrough.

I hope that this book has inspired you to feel like you are an IN-Powered woman. It is my hope that you have everything that it takes to be powerful, successful, loving, connected and supportive. Embody this concept and be her every day that you are alive and breathing.

As Gandhi once said, "Be the change that you wish to see in the world." It's beautiful to have your eyes open so that you can uncover a power that's been in you all along. Together, we IN-Powered women can conquer and create together. Step into your power now, and let's change the world one day at a time.

# THE IN-POWERED WOMAN

# About The Author

Nikkie Pryce also known as the "self-love influencer", bestselling author and prominent transformational life coach and women's speaker are a global force to be reckoned with.

With a strong focus on inspiring and motivating women to put action behind their dreams, Nikkie is the Founder and Leader of I AM Community, a women's empowerment organization that has helped thousands of women improve their mental health wellness, self-esteem, and self-confidence through I AM affirmations.

Nikkie's book, Dreamers, Take Action! Has changed the lives of dreamers worldwide. She has empowered dozens of women to take action towards their dreams of becoming published authors in less than 90 days through her coaching program. It is because of her love for women's empowerment that she was nominated as Woman of The Year by HerNetwork, a global women's empowerment organization in Lagos, Nigeria.

Nikkie has been featured in national publications

such as The Huffington Post and Voyager online magazine as a trailblazer with an inspiring story. Nikkie has also been seen on the ABC network, where she started her career in production and reporting.

She has partnered with companies such as Verizon and WeWork to produce impactful and inspiring women's empowerment events. She is a community-driven leader whose give-back initiatives provided over 200+ school supplies, lunches and empowerment workshops to inner-city youth for the Boys & Girls Club in New York City.

Having spoken and taught her signature Self-Love workshop for the Miami Dolphins Cheerleaders and Miami Heat Dancers, Nikkie is a certified Health Minister who is equipped to coach and teach health and mental wellness strategies in communities and congregations.

www.nikkiepryce.com  nikkie@nikkiepryce.com
Follow Nikkie on Instagram: @IAMNikkiePryce

# THE IN-POWERED WOMAN

Made in the USA
Middletown, DE
13 February 2022

61079615R00060